D0678994

ORAL HISTORY
FOR THE LOCAL HISTORICAL SOCIETY

AMERICAN ASSOCIATION FOR STATE AND LOCAL HISTORY BOOK SERIES

Series Editor

Sandra Sageser Clark
Michigan Historical Center

Editorial Advisory Board

Robert R. Archibald, Missouri Historical Society
Charles F. Bryan, Jr., Virginia Historical Society
Lonnie G. Bunch, Smithsonian Institution
George F. MacDonald, Canadian Museum of Civilization
George L. Vogt, South Carolina Department of Archives and History

About the Series:

The American Association for State and Local History Book Series publishes technical and professional information for those who practice and support history and addresses issues critical to the field of state and local history. To submit a proposal or manuscript to the series, please request proposal guidelines from AASLH headquarters: AASLH Book Series, 530 Church Street, Suite 600, Nashville, Tennessee 37219. Telephone: (615) 255-2971. Fax: (615) 255-2979.

About the Organization:

The American Association for State and Local History (AASLH) is a non-profit educational organization dedicated to advancing knowledge, understanding, and appreciation of local history in the United States and Canada. In addition to sponsorship of this book series, the association publishes the periodical HISTORY NEWS, a newsletter, technical leaflets and reports, and other materials; confers prizes and awards in recognition of outstanding achievement in the field; and supports a broad educational program and other activities designed to help members work more effectively. Current members are entitled to discounts on AASLH Series books. To join the organization, contact the Membership Director, AASLH, 530 Church Street, Suite 600, Nashville, Tennessee 37219.

Oral History for the Local Historical Society

Third Edition, Revised

WILLA K. BAUM

ALTAMIRA
PRESS

A Division of
ROWMAN & LITTLEFIELD PUBLISHERS, INC.
Walnut Creek • Lanham • New York • Oxford

907.2
B3270

OIL CITY LIBRARY
2 CENTRAL AVENUE
OIL CITY, PA. 16301

ALTAMIRA PRESS
A Division of Rowman & Littlefield Publishers, Inc.
1630 North Main Street, #367
Walnut Creek, CA 94596
www.altamirapress.com

Rowman & Littlefield Publishers, Inc.
4720 Boston Way
Lanham, MD 20706

12 Hid's Copse Road
Cumnor Hill, Oxford OX2 9JJ, England

Copyright © 1995 by AltaMira Press

Copyright © 1967, 1971, 1987 by Willa K. Baum

All rights reserved. No part of this publication may be reproduced,
stored in a retrieval system, or transmitted in any form or by any
means, electronic, mechanical, photocopying, recording, or otherwise,
without the prior permission of the publisher.

British Library Cataloguing in Publication Information Available

Library of Congress Cataloging-in-Publication Data

Baum, Willa K.
   Oral history for the local historical society / Willa K. Baum — 3rd ed., rev.
   p. cm.—(American Association for State and Local History book series)
   Originally published: Nashville, Tenn. : American Association for State and
   Local History, 1987. 3rd ed., rev.
   Includes bibliographical references and index.
   ISBN 0-7619-9133-6
   1. Oral History. I. Title. II. Series.
D16.14.B37 1995
907'.2—dc20   95-42556
                                                                CIP

Printed in the United States of America

♾™ The paper used in this publication meets the minimum requirements of American
National Standard for Information Sciences—Permanence of Paper for Printed Library
Materials, ANSI/NISO Z39.48–1992.

Designed by Gillian Murrey. Originally published by the American Association for State
and Local History.

The publisher wishes to thank the Oral History Project of the Country Music Foundation
in Nashville, Tennessee, for providing equipment to update photographs in this revised
edition. Thanks also to Angelia Gacesa and John Rumble of the Country Music
Foundation for their help with the equioment. Photographs on pages 8, 11, 13, 17, 19,
20, 22, 26, 27, 29, 31, 33, 40, 43, 46, 50, 59, and 61 by Henry Murrey.

Contents

Note on the Author

Willa K. Baum is director of the Regional Oral History Office at the University of California, Berkeley, a position she has held since 1954. She has played a major role in developing the techniques of oral history with *Oral History for the Local Historical Society*, 1969; *Transcribing and Editing Oral History*, 1977; and *Oral History: An Interdisciplinary Anthology*, (with David K. Dunaway) 1984, all published by AASLH. Baum is a past council member of the Oral History Association and a former oral history committee member of the Society of American Archivists.

Foreword

In 1969 the Conference of California Historical Societies published the first edition of Willa Baum's *Oral History for the Local Historical Society*. The second edition, published by the American Association for State and Local History in 1971, introduced the booklet to a wider audience. It was an immediate success because of the expertise of its nationally recognized author and her ability to discuss a somewhat technical subject in easily understood terms. The booklet answered well a growing need of historical societies for help in establishing oral history programs.

Subsequently, that need has continued to grow, partly because the number of historical societies has continued to grow phenomenally, and partly because oral history has vastly increased both in popularity and in respect as a valuable source of historical understanding. The demand for Willa Baum's basic little book has continued unabated through the 1970s and 1980s. Hundreds of historical organizations have now built significant oral history programs on its principles. Hundreds of individual historians have used Willa Baum's guidance to "do right" a form of research that is not as simple as it might seem.

The American Association for State and Local History is now delighted to publish this new, revised, third edition of Willa Baum's classic handbook. She has brought its recommendations up-to-date, and we have added new illustrations and a new format as well. Thus we hope to continue into the 1990s and beyond the sound influence of a book that already has contributed so much to the oral history movement throughout North America.

GERALD GEORGE
Director, AASLH
1987

Preface to the 1987 edition

Almost twenty years have passed since I first put together *Oral History for the Local Historical Society*. The oral history scene has expanded since those early days; there are more oral history projects, more manuals on how to do it, more published books based on oral history, and more associations and workshops.

But essentially the method is the same; the steps described in 1969 still work as well, as attested to by hundreds of oral history interviewers who followed the book to the successful completion of their projects. And so basically I have left the book as it was drafted in that Bicentennial decade as an answer to the groups besieging our office for advice.

There were some revisions that were essential, however. First, equipment. The debate over reel-to-reel or cassette recorders has been settled, I think unfortunately, by the marketplace. There are almost no reel-to-reel recorders available, and so tape recorder means cassette recorder. The equipment advice has been updated.

There were sample questions that had to be revised—the narrators who could recall many of the events we asked about in the 1960s are gone, and so we must go after more recent history. After all, oral history is about events and ways of life within the memory of the narrator.

There are many more books, newsletters, and associations available to help the serious oral historian do a better job. A selected few have been added to the bibliography.

Lastly, the women's movement has brought about a change in writing style. We can no longer use the masculine pronoun for everyman or everywoman singular. Until the English language produces a new neuter singular pronoun, writers must retreat into passive voice, or plural actors, or bifurcated s/he. Rather than write 'He or she gives his or her transcript to him or her." I have set up an arbitrary situation. For general examples, all narrators will be "she" and all the interviewing staff will be "he," pronouns which here denote function rather than gender. For specific examples, the narrator will be male or female as the case may be.

Otherwise, *Oral History for the Local Historical Society* remains the same basic guide for carrying out a modest ongoing program for documenting history from the accounts of persons who have lived it.

WILLA K. BAUM
1987

What Is Oral History?

The way of life that was characteristic of an earlier America is rapidly
disappearing, but there are persons still alive today who remember it
vividly. It is unlikely that they will preserve their pioneer memories
by writing memoirs, as historians would wish them to do, but many
old-timers are willing to tell their stories and confide their
reminiscences to tape recordings. Likewise busy citizens immersed in
economic, political, or civic activities today may be willing to set
aside time to tape-record the whys and hows of their efforts in order
to preserve a more current history of the community. While the
individual recordings are sometimes fragmentary and highly
personal, taken together they provide a fund of color, detail, and
incident invaluable for future historical research.

Oral history is the tape-recording of reminiscences about which the
narrator can speak from first-hand knowledge. Through pre-planned
interviews, the information is captured in question and answer form
by oral history interviewers. The interviewer must have some
background knowledge of the subject and considerable social skill in
knowing how to draw the narrator out. Oral history is not the tape-
recording of speeches or other community events, although this
should be another part of the historical society's collecting program.

Oral history interviews differ from journalistic or specific historical
research interviews in that they are intended for use in the future by
a wide variety of researchers; therefore their scope should be broader
than what would be covered for immediate or specific use. A plan for
preservation and use is essential to oral history.

Why Oral History?

Local historical societies have assumed the responsibility of preserving the history of their communities. In this effort they engage in collecting, preserving, and making available for research manuscripts relating to the community, such as diaries, letters, and business and civic records. They preserve the implements and photographs of life in a bygone era and often establish museums so that these may be seen by the public. Historic sites are preserved or reconstructed and maintained for public viewing. Through a publications program or a lecture program, the historical society

stimulates historical research and the dissemination of the results of that research.

Oral history is a relatively new and increasingly essential part of the efforts of the local historical society. In this day of hurried contacts, telephones, or face-to-face meetings, and multitudinous evening activities, people no longer write the long letters, the routinely kept diaries, the series of letters back and forth to work out an agreement, the careful memos that heretofore have always served as the bones of historical research. And, as always, there are many classes of people who will not set down in writing the description of their way of life although they may have a very rich oral tradition and may be able to talk with much color and accuracy about this life.

These gaps can now be filled by oral history. Through the relatively painless medium of relaxed conversations based upon well-planned questions, it is possible to elicit information that would not ordinarily get into the written record: the descriptions of the appearance and character of leading citizens, the motivations as to why and how and by what "gentleman's agreement" things came to pass, the life and color of a community or an industry or an ethnic group.

In addition to providing research information, oral history can serve as a link from the immediate present to the immediate past in an understandable and very human way that can give the young and the newcomers a way of sinking their roots into the community.

Most importantly (because local historical societies are manned by volunteer workers), oral history can be fun for the interviewer, the narrator, and anyone else concerned with the work.

How to Start an
Oral History Program

Set Up a Committee

Start with a small group of members of the historical society who have indicated an interest in collecting the history of this century. The number of your committee, their individual interests, and the time they have available for this work will indicate how extensive an oral history program you should plan.

Make Preliminary Plans:
Who Should Be Interviewed?

It is usually recommended that you organize a community survey by which you establish what the major community developments of interest have been, what recorded information on them already exists, what people are available who can tell about these things, and then in what priority they should be interviewed. It has been my observation, however, that such a survey takes too long, that as a result part of your interested group will drop out before you are ready to begin interviewing, and that several of your prime prospective narrators will die or become incapacitated while you are considering.

At the risk of sounding unprofessional, I recommend that you immediately decide upon three or four persons to be interviewed who are known to the group for their first-hand knowledge of community developments, and that you begin the interviewing program without delay. At the same time, you may conduct the community survey. Your whole program will develop and change as you go. Often the best sources of information on whom to interview will be your narrators themselves.

In deciding whom to start with, take into consideration factors of age and health. Actuarial statistics will give some of your prospective narrators only a slim chance of being here next year. Don't be afraid to start with them. If you do a poor job due to inexperience, wait six

4

months, and then go back and do the interviews over if the narrator is still able. If not, console yourself that a poor interview is better than none.

At the same time as you are beginning the interviewing program, you can be preparing a list of topics to be covered in the interviews, and a list of additional potential narrators. A brief notice in the local paper to the effect that the society is gathering information on "the history of Valley County since 1930" or "the history of the schools in Valley County since 1930," and that you would appreciate having the names of people who might be able to tell about that subject, will give you some leads.

Do not indicate that you intend to interview these people on tape, either in a newspaper account or in a preliminary letter or by any other way. You will soon have far too many names, so do not commit yourself until you have had a chance to evaluate the prospective narrator, and until you know how much work your committee can handle.

Consider a Questionnaire

It is often helpful to prepare a questionnaire that can be used to help you decide whom to call on personally; if you decide to interview the person, the questionnaire can be the beginning of an

outline for this interview. The questionnaire must be designed to fit
your own topics.

Here is a sample questionnaire that proved very useful to a
volunteer oral history committee working on the history of a college
women's society. In keeping with a policy of getting the oldest first,
the questionnaire was sent to all pre-1920 alumnae, and from the
answers a list of narrators was prepared.

Prytanean Society Oral History Questionnaire

Name _____

Class _____

Maiden Name _____

No. of Children _____

Address _____

Phone _____

Birthplace _____

Why did you go to the University of California _____

_____

What was your major? _____

What were your extracurricular activities? _____

_____

What were some of the things that Prytanean did while you were on campus?

_____

Did you prepare yourself for a profession _____

If so, which one? _____

Did you actually work in this profession (or some other)? _____

Please give brief details _____

Do you feel that your college work helped to prepare you for the life you have actually lived?

_____

How would you have changed your preparation if you could have looked into the future?

_____

List some of your most significant "extracurricular" or civic activities since graduation

_____

What has been your participation in Prytanean Alumnae affairs? _____

_____

What has been your participation in University Alumni affairs? _____

_____

☐ I should be glad to have a volunteer interviewer talk with me about my recollection of
the Prytanean Society. I am available except as noted below:

Prepare a General List of Questions

The outline for every person's interview will have to be prepared separately and should be based on that person's career or vantage point in the events you are inquiring about. However, there will be general questions that you will ask all the narrators—some biographical, some topical.

Biographically, you will want to establish the individual's identity. Depending on your purposes, this may be answered in five minutes or in one or two interviews. The questions should include father's and mother's names and a little on their background, such as where they came from, and something about their occupations. For genealogical purposes, more information on the family tree may be sought. (Since this is hard to keep track of verbally and takes much time, the narrator might be willing to prepare a family chart in writing to be added to the file.) Then, of course, the narrator's birthdate and birthplace, education, travels, occupation, spouse, and children.

Topically, there will be major national and community events you will ask about, such as the Depression, World War II, the 1949 tornado, and the opening of the freeway in 1955. Good general references for this kind of information are college history textbooks and your own state, county, and city histories.

From these, and from histories of the topics you may be investigating (i.e. livestock, mining, seafaring), you should be able to draw up a general list of important events to ask about. From there on, it is the responsibility of each interviewer to tailor-make the interview outlines to the individual narrators.

Print Stationery or Calling Cards

It should always be clear to the people from whom you collect historical materials that this is a historical society endeavor, not an individual endeavor, even though the oral history committee may be a committee of one. People you deal with should have in writing the name of the society and of the person they are talking to.

Most historical societies have letterhead stationery already printed, and this should be used for all official communications about interviews. If there is no stationery, the oral history committee should have some printed. If the program will be a substantial one with many contacts with the public, calling cards should be printed, identifying the historical society and providing a blank area that members of the committee can use to fill in their own names. This card should be given to people you call on in person for information or for historical papers; a confirming letter on historical society letterhead should follow.

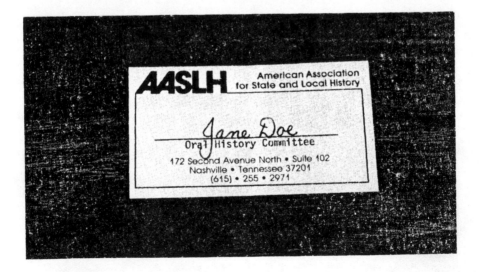

Equipment and Tapes

One of the nice things about oral history is that the equipment required is so inexpensive and so readily available. Cost for a tape recorder plus tapes will be under $300, under $150 in some instances. Special transcribing equipment will cost more, but it is not necessary in the beginning. Plan to buy your equipment at a local electronics shop that has a reputation for standing behind its products and for handling repairs competently.

Tape Recorders

If you appoint a committee to select a tape recorder, you will naturally put on it your most knowledgeable person on electronics. Be sure also to include on the committee several people who will be using the recorder but who have no mechanical talents. The recorder chosen must be one they will be comfortable with, as well as one that is satisfactory to the high-fidelity buff.

It is difficult to advise on equipment as the market is in constant flux. Since the previous edition of this manual, the favorite field recorders of most oral historians (for example, the Sony TC 100 and the Marantz Superscope C-200) have been taken out of production, and the market has shifted to either very high-fidelity studio equipment or entertainment equipment emphasizing radio and cassette playback. It can be expected that new models of field recorders will come on the market.

Here I will discuss the considerations to hold in mind and some features to look for in selecting equipment. My recommendations are aimed at the program that has interviewers who do not use the equipment often enough to become comfortable with monitoring and adjusting the recorder. Therefore, the advantage of good sound quality has to be balanced against the need for simplicity of operation and minimal chance of error. If you want broadcast-quality recording, refer to some of the manuals listed in the bibliography that emphasize recording technique.

Considerations:

1. Ease of operation: Can you set up and monitor the machine while conducting the interview?
2. Sound fidelity: Can the recorded voices be understood?
3. Reliability: Does the machine record when you expect it to?
4. Ease of maintenance: Is the machine sturdy with a low repair record?

Until recently the first decision was whether to use reel-to-reel or cassette equipment, with moderately priced, easy-to-operate recorders of suitable quality available in either format. Unfortunately, reel-to-reel equipment has virtually disappeared from the market place except for the very professional and excellent Uhrer 4000 series and the Nagra field recorders, either of which would cost more than a thousand dollars. This discussion will be limited to less expensive cassette equipment.

Your electronics dealer can show you cassette tape recorders with a variety of features. Remember, though, that the more features a recorder has, the higher the cost and the closer attention you must pay to the techniques of recording. It is easy to be persuaded by dealers (who feel very comfortable around electronic equipment, else they would have gone into some other business) that making a few extra adjustments as you set up the recorder will not be beyond your capacity. What dealers will not realize is that you will have so many things to think about in starting an interview that you can forget one of those adjustments and lose your whole recording.

Features:

Size. Larger field recorders will be more rugged. Look for a machine of between five and eight pounds in weight with a metal case that is screwed together so that it can be opened and repaired. (An added boon is that larger machines are less often stolen than are small ones.)

Power. A field recorder should be able to operate on both AC current and DC batteries. Plan to use AC current when it is available to avoid the problems of uneven recording speed that come with fading batteries. But be prepared to switch to batteries if there seems to be interference in the sound—main current sometimes surges, or carries radio waves, or hums, all of which can diminish the fidelity of the sound recording. In some machines, the AC/DC capability is built in;

in others, using AC current may require an additional purchase of a cord and convertor to plug into the main line. Alkaline batteries are better than carbon-zinc batteries; they last longer, leak less, recover more quickly, and cost more. A rechargeable nickel-cadmium battery pack may prove an economy if battery power is used often.

Operation. All switches should work smoothly and all plugs fit snugly, as wobbly plugs can cause you to lose portions of the interview. The control panel should be easy to read with buttons and switches in logical places. The cassettes should fit into the cassette compartment firmly, but eject smoothly.

Microphone jack. Be sure the tape recorder has a jack for an external microphone. An oral historian should never use built-in mikes. They are inferior mikes, and the sound they pick up best is the sound of the recorder motor. All but the cheapest machines have microphone jacks.

Two or three heads. This choice involves the ability to monitor the sound either before it is recorded or after it is recorded. Less expensive recorders have two heads, the first to erase the tape, the second to record and to play back. This is all you need for recording. However, when the second head is recording, it cannot play back. Therefore, with a two-head machine if you monitor the tape, what you will hear is the sound that is going into the machine. You may not hear additional sounds that are being recorded—for example, radio waves from the main current—and you will not know if the recording head is malfunctioning and nothing is being recorded. With the more expensive three-head machines, the third head is playback, and you can monitor what has been recorded. If the interviewers are willing to monitor now and then during the interview (that is, listen with a little earphone), then three heads are better and may save you some defective recordings.

Manual level control or automatic level control. Recording level control is adjustment of the the sound level so it will be recorded with the least amount of noise and distortion. Automatic level control (ALC) automatically adjusts the sound level; when voices or background sound go up, the ALC adjusts the level downward, resulting in a tape of undifferentiated sound level—less noise distortion, but also less sound dynamics and less interesting and accurate sound and background ambience. Manual level control with a VU meter (volume unit) requires the interviewer to adjust the sound level to the voice and sound situation before beginning the interview; manual level control will provide more accurate sound dynamics, but occasional noise distortion. Less expensive machines have only ALC; more expensive machines offer ALC and manual level control; a few offer ALC and manual level control plus a limiter, which prevents the recording level from jumping up to the distortion level. If the inter-viewers can deal with adjusting the sound level, and watching the VU meter, and with occasionally monitoring, I recommend the use of manual level control with a limiter. However, ALC does an adequate job with no adjustments necessary.

Mono or stereo. Mono records one track from one mike. Generally, the mike is placed to pick up the narrator's voice, and the interviewer has to speak up to be heard. Stereo makes separate recording on two tracks from two microphones. On the plus side, stereo sound is fuller; the narrator and interviewer each have a mike for which separate levels can be set to match each one's voice. But stereo requires two microphones, more adjusting, and it costs more. I recommend against using stereo unless sound quality is of prime concern, (for example, for tapes used in radio broadcasts).

There are other options: adjustments for tape types, noise reduc-tion systems, variable playback speeds, and variable recording speeds. They have advantages, they cost more, they are not necessary, and you may not be able to use them. Don't buy beyond the technical skills of your interviewers.

Microphones

Good sound fidelity requires a good microphone. Do not use the built-in microphone. Select your external mike when you select the tape recorder—the mike and the recorder must match plug sizes and inpedances; in fact, you cannot test the sound capacity of the tape recorder except with a good microphone. In testing tape recorders with microphones, remember that it is recording quality you are looking for, not playback. An excellent field recorder may have a minimal speaker system so that playback on that machine may not be a true test of its recording capacity.

The microphone should be directional, called "cardiod pick-up," which focuses on sounds in front of the mike. Omnidirectional mikes pick up sound equally in all directions, increasing the likelihood of getting distracting environmental sounds. A directional mike, assuming you use only one mike aimed at the narrator, requires the interviewer to speak up loudly. This should discourage the interviewer from any excess verbiage, an advantage in itself.

The microphone can be a stand-up mike, requiring a table stand or a floor stand, or a lavalier mike, which clips onto the lapel or hangs around the neck of the interviewee. For best pick up, the mike should be positioned from six to eighteen inches from the speaker's mouth.

A lavalier mike is most convenient. It is always close to the speaker and pointed in the right direction. However, there are some inconveniences. The mike requires a tiny hearing-aid battery, which should be removed between uses. This means inserting the battery each time you use the mike, checking to be sure it is working, and having an extra battery along in case it fades. It also means monitoring, listening to what is coming in the machine, which you can do on both the two-head and the three-head recorders. The little batteries last a long time, but when they go, they go without warning, possibly leaving you with only the memory of a wonderful interview that is not recorded.

A stand-up mike is larger and does not need its own battery. It is mounted on either a table-top stand or a floor stand. A floor stand with a boom is best for sound; the mike can be positioned properly for speakers no matter where they sit, and as it is suspended in the air from the floor base, it is less likely to pick up sounds such as objects being moved around on a table. A floor stand is a cumbersome piece of equipment to carry and set up. A table stand is a smaller piece of equipment, but it is hard to position close enough to the speaker. A table stand mike should be placed on a rubber pad or cushion to reduce vibration.

I recommend using the lavalier mike with a fresh battery.

Cassette Tapes

Cassette tapes are small, convenient to use, and they offer excellent storage protection. They usually come in a plastic or paper box ready for labeling. An even greater joy to the oral historian is the fact that two little holes in the back of the cassette can be pushed out, after which the recording heads will no longer engage the tape. By doing this the tape can be played over and over but cannot be accidentally erased.

Recording the spoken voice does not require the sound range that music does, so you do not need the highest-priced tapes. Any medium-priced standard brand of cassette tape such as Ampex, Scotch, TDK, BASF, or Maxell, is adequate. Buy the thickest tape available, C-60s, which means thirty minutes of recording per side for

a total of sixty minutes. Do not use C-90s or C-120s. These longer playing cassettes use thinner tapes. Thicker tapes preserve the sound better and longer and are less likely to tangle, stretch, or "bleed through" (the recording signal fades into the adjacent tape, creating an "echo" affect.) Cassette cases that are screwed together rather than welded are preferable as they can be opened if it is necessary to untangle or repair the tape.

Recorder Maintenance Equipment:

A tape recorder with dirty heads will produce a poor tape or, on playback, damage a tape. Tape heads should be cleaned after eight to ten hours of recording, and the recorder should be demagnetized once a month. For cleaning, you need cotton Q-tips and isopropyl alcohol; for demagnetizing you need a demagnetizing cassette or a degaussing wand.

The Interview Process

Contacting the Narrator

Call or write the prospective narrator indicating that you are surveying sources of information on the history of the community (or whatever your theme may be) and would like to talk to her about this. Do not bring up the oral history aspect at this time. When you meet, inquire about her background and take notes on her biographical data; find out if she has or knows of papers or other materials of historical significance. In the course of the conversation, you will be getting the material you need to prepare interview outlines, and you will be able to evaluate her personally as a prospective narrator. Depending on your committee's plans, you may decide then and there to interview her and immediately invite her to participate; or you may take the information back to the committee and use it as a basis for establishing a narrator list.

Explaining the Program to the Narrator

The invitation to participate can come personally or by letter. In either event, you should explain what the purpose is and how the interviewing will proceed. Answer questions such as: Where will the tapes be kept when the interviewing is finished? Who may use them and under what circumstances? May the narrator get a copy of the tape for herself? How many sessions do you plan? (Always start with far fewer sessions than you expect to do. It is easy to decide to do more as you proceed; it is almost impossible to lower the number of sessions you suggest originally.)

At the Bancroft Library, we usually explain the project, then follow up with a letter reiterating the plan, and ask the narrator to sign and return a carbon copy of this letter if it meets her approval. We feel it helps to avoid misunderstandings if all parties concerned have a clear and permanent record of what they have agreed upon.

Central City Historical Society

85 Main Street
Central City, Missouri

Mrs. Althea Johnson
1220 Pine St.
Central City

Dear Mrs. Johnson:

Last week Mr. John Allen of the Central City Historical Society called on you regarding the Central City Y.W.C.A. This letter is to invite you to be a narrator in our oral history program of documenting the history of Central City. We would like to record your recollections of your many years of work with the Y.W.C.A., and of any other social agencies that you dealt with.

The interview will be held in your home or any other place convenient for you. The interview is a conversation in which you will be asked about the things you did, the people you knew, and the events you observed.

The tapes, and a transcript of the tapes if funding permits, will be placed in the Central City Library for users to listen to. You will receive a copy of the tapes for your personal files.

The purpose of the project is to make the information available to researchers. At the conclusion of the interview you will be asked to sign an agreement opening your oral history to use.

Our interviewer John Allen will call you to discuss topics to be covered in the interview and to set up a convenient interviewing time for you.

I am enclosing a copy of this letter for you to sign and return to me if these arrangements meet with your approval.

Sincerely yours,

(Mrs.) Grace Nielson
Chair, Oral History Committee

Approved:

_____

Mrs. Althea Johnson

_____

Date

A Planning Session with the Narrator

Talk over with the narrator the subjects you will discuss in the course of the interviews. The biographical data she has already given you will be your first guideline. She may suggest topics she knows a lot about; you will ask her if she knows about others as well; plan together what you will include in the recordings.

A common problem in this planning session is to keep the conversation on what you *will* talk about, but without getting into the details right then. The information you will get on the tape will be much fresher and livelier if she hasn't told you the story already at the planning session. Avoiding this can be very difficult, and it is a good idea to plan a short session and inform your narrator ahead of time that you have an unbreakable appointment in an hour. For the very loquacious narrator, you may need a definite time when you must leave after each interview.

Preparing Interview Outlines

At home you will prepare a very general outline of what you plan to talk about for the entire course of interviews, plus a more specific

Kringle, John P.   April 17, 1987
Session #1

I. Early life in Central City
   A. Family background
   B. Education
      1. Attended area's last one-room
         school
      2. Banking apprenticeship
   C. First job as bank clerk

II. Banking career
   A. Reaction of C.C. banks to war-time
      economy
   B. C.C. banks during Great Depression
   C. Merger of Trust Co. with Bank
      of America
   D. Move into present bank
      headquarters

Topic for session #2
   Kringle's term on city council

outline of the first interview. Keep this in brief outline form. *Do not* word the questions. For example, write in your outline, "Father's background—parents, school, occupation," not "What was your father's name? What was his occupation?" A question written previously will sound like a canned speech when you read it and will destroy the informality of your interview.

Most interviewees appreciate receiving a copy of the interview outline a few days before the session; for a few, this is just a worry. Every step of the way you will have to adjust what you do to what works best with a specific narrator.

Remind the Narrator of the Interview Appointment

Whether you do or don't send an outline, do drop the narrator a line or telephone her a few days before the scheduled taping session as a reminder of the time, date, and topics you will be discussing. This will encourage the narrator to refresh her memory by looking over her papers, talking to her spouse, or just ruminating.

Practice with the Tape Recorder Beforehand

If you are not thoroughly familiar with the tape recorder, practice at home setting it up and putting it away so this will not cause you any concern. Using your family or a friend as a foil, practice casually setting up the machine, including crawling under tables in search of electrical outlets while carrying on a conversation. Become proficient at it; you will have too many other things to think about at the time of the first interview to have to worry about the machine.

Plan a Formal Introduction to the Tape

Plan to include on the tape a formal introduction that gives the place and date, the narrator's name, and briefly who he or she is, and who you are. For example: "This is an interview with John P. Kringle, retired banker of the Central City Trust Company of Central City. Mr. Kringle has been a banker since 1932, having worked through the Great Depression and the effects of the Bank Holiday, World War II, the land boom of the 1950s, and the absorption of the Central City Trust Company into the Bank of America in 1962. This interview is being conducted on April 17, 1987, at Mr. Kringle's home

on East Hampton Street. The interviewer is William Smith, representing the Central City Historical Society."

Practice this introduction on the tape and determine how much tape it will take. Be prepared to "fast forward" to that point in the tape when you are ready to begin recording the interview.

But do not record the introduction beforehand, or your narrator may hear it as you try the recording out. As a general practice, do not read the introduction into the tape when you start the interview. There is nothing that can give a timid narrator mike-fright more surely than for you to speak a formal introduction and then let her know that she is "on the air."

On the other hand, you may be working with a narrator who tends to exaggerate or to make reckless statements about her associates—statements that she may regret later or which might damage the community. A judicious reminder in the form of a formal introduction on the tape may alert the narrator to the fact that this is a permanent, public document. One must consider how to work with each narrator and each situation individually.

Starting the Interview: Setting Up the Equipment

Arrive at the appointed time.

Situate the interview where there will be as few interruptions as possible. Discourage the presence of a third party, especially a husband or wife. (Interview spouses separately if they can add to the account.)

Be sure the narrator is comfortable. Don't let her give you her favorite chair.

After you have determined where you will sit, locate the recorder where you can watch it. If you use a lavalier mike, clip it to the narrator, reminding her that she is now attached and cannot jump up and walk across the room to get something. If you use a stand-up mike, position it on a table stand or floor stand within eighteen inches of the narrator. Never put the mike and the recorder on the same table. A pad under a table mike will cut down on vibration noise.

Establishing Rapport

Turn on the machine immediately, and let it run while you chat a bit about the weather. Be relaxed and show no concern for the passage of tape. Your narrator may want to ask a few more questions. You may wish to remind her of the purpose of the recording. Tell her you will be taking notes on names and places and dates she mentions, and you hope she will check the spellings after the interview. While you are chatting, casually rewind the tape and play it back, making sure the volume is adjusted to pick up her voice clearly and yours also. She will probably be interested in the sound of her voice on the tape, and you can listen to a little of what you have recorded. Then go back to the point on the tape where you planned to begin.

Turn on the recorder, settle back, and slide into your first question easily. "Mrs. Johnson, before we get into the early days of the Central

City Y.W.C.A., would you tell me something about yourself? Where and when were you born?"

Be interested. Listen to what your narrator is saying, and make the appropriate comments. Do not be so concerned about your next question that when she stops for air, you blurt it out. She may not have finished what she was saying. This does not apply if she is very long-winded and you are trying to hustle her along into the next subject.

Taking Notes

Keep running notes on names, places, and dates she may mention. These will be of help to the person who listens to the tape at a later date and to you when you prepare an index of the tape. Most importantly, it will give you something to do during the long pauses when you do not want to stare silently into the narrator's eyes, nor want to speak before she has completed her thought. The most common error of the beginning interviewer is jumping into every silence with the next question. Taking notes will help prevent this and will also permit you to check spellings with your narrator at the close of the interview. Most narrators are flattered to think that you consider what they are saying important enough to be making notes.

Turning the Tape

Depending on the length of the tape, you will run out in thirty minutes or forty-five minutes. As this time approaches, try to find a natural place to break before the tape runs out. If your narrator seems a little tired, this is the time either to suggest that you leave and come back next week or that this is a convenient time to take a break. If you turn the tape and continue after a break, slide into the topic again. "You were telling about the services the YWCA provided for women shipyard workers. How did that affect your job?"

Closing the Interview

An hour and a half is usually the maximum length for an interview session. Although some narrators can go longer without fatigue, the interviewer usually cannot. One is often tempted to get just one more good story on the tape before turning off the recorder, but a few experiences of having the narrator (or spouse) call and cancel the next appointment because it is just too fatiguing will prove the folly of this plan.

Set the time limit in your own mind, then stop at an appropriate break in the story near that time. Explain that you must be leaving shortly. Ask the narrator to check over the spelling of the names in your notes while you pack up the recorder. Spend a few minutes planning what you will discuss next time. Perhaps she will lend you a scrapbook or some mementos that will help you prepare the questions for next week. Try to leave no more than half an hour after the close of the recording; otherwise you will hear all the stories she is going to tell you next week.

Homework after the Interview

Shortly after the interview, prepare the tape for permanent record. Right after the interview, place a label on the box and on the cassette itself, with the name of narrator and interviewer, the date, and the length of time of the recording. If this is a second or later interview, you should also indicate what number interview it is.

Record your introduction onto the lead-in tape at the front of the cassette.

Having thus properly identified the tape, listen through it and prepare the tape index (see the section on indexing). Note topics that need to be discussed further at the next recording session. Then listen through the tape again for your own training (see the section on developing expertise).

Collecting Other Materials

The value of the oral history information will be enhanced if you can collect other illustrative materials. The narrator may have letters, clippings, reports, photographs, printed programs, or other items that would be useful to the researcher. These should be collected if possible and filed with the tapes, or in separate files but cross-catalogued. Try to get a photograph of the narrator at the time of the interview, even if you have to take along your own camera to do it.

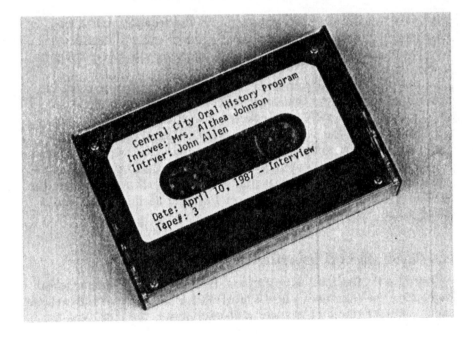

Who Should Interview?

As in any art, interviewing can be done in many ways by many different sorts of people, and although the results may be different, they can all be good. The very friendly, informal person will interview in one way; the more formal, correct, and controlled person will interview in another way. The interviewer should be someone who can sit quietly and listen, who is willing to let the narrator express an opinion contrary to his own without feeling compelled to contradict or re-educate the narrator, who is not afraid to break in occasionally with a question or guiding comment, who is firm enough to end the interview on time and to keep it within the bounds of whatever lines of inquiry have been planned, who is alert enough and knowledgeable enough to recognize when the narrator brings up an unplanned but valuable subject, and who is able to pursue that new subject with questions.

There are, however, two types of people who should not be assigned to interviewing. They are the compulsive talker and the compulsive director. Both types will end up with interviews of themselves. The compulsive talker will do most of the talking, in the guise of lengthy questions or comments between brief yeses or noes of the narrator. The compulsive director will be able to guide the narrator into telling what the interviewer thinks is the appropriate account, much to the later dissatisfaction of the narrator and the nonvalidity of the historical information. So use the director-type to head up the program, and the talker-type to publicize the program, to raise funds for equipment, and to put the information that is obtained into use through lectures. Save the interviewing itself for the quieter people in the group.

A well-organized oral history program encompasses such a variety of activities that almost every personality type can make a satisfying contribution to the program. The very shy person who may feel uncomfortable interviewing may be ideal to keep the tape files organized, to index the tapes, to send information on the interviews to the state library, and to do transcribing if that is decided upon. The mechanically inclined may be prevailed upon to branch out and

record other events such as major addresses or other important happenings. Ideally one member of the group will have the administrative skill to guide people into the right jobs for them.

Tips for Interviewers

1. An interview is not a dialogue. The whole point of the interview is to get the narrator to tell her story. Limit your own remarks to a few pleasantries to break the ice, then brief questions to guide her along. It is not necessary to give her the details of your great-grandmother's trip in a covered wagon in order to get her to tell you about her grandfather's trip to California. Just say, "I understand your grandfather came around the Horn to California. What did he tell you about the trip?"

2. Ask questions that require more of an answer than "yes" or "no." Start with "why," how," where," "what kind of. . ." Instead of "Was Henry Miller a good boss?" ask "What did the cowhands think of Henry Miller as a boss?"

3. Ask one question at a time. Sometimes interviewers ask a series a questions all at once. Probably the narrator will answer only the first or last one. You will catch this kind of questioning when you listen through the tape after the session, and you can avoid it the next time.

4. Ask brief questions. We all know the irrepressible speech-maker who, when questions are called for at the end of a lecture, gets up and asks five-minute questions. It is unlikely that the narrator is so dull that it takes more than a sentence or two for her to understand the question.

5. Start with questions that are not controversial; save the delicate questions, if there are any, until you have become better acquainted. A good place to begin is with the narrator's youth and background.

6. Don't let periods of silence fluster you. Give your narrator a chance to think of what she wants to add before you hustle her along with the next question. Relax, write a few words on your notepad. The sure sign of a beginning interviewer is a tape where every brief pause signals the next question.

7. Don't worry if your questions are not as beautifully phrased as you would like them to be for posterity. A few fumbled questions will help put your narrator at ease as she realizes that you are not perfect and she need not worry if she isn't either. It is not necessary

to practice fumbling a few questions; most of us are nervous enough to do that naturally.

8. Don't interrupt a good story because you have thought of a question, or because your narrator is straying from the planned outline. If the information is pertinent, let her go on, but jot down your question on your notepad so you will remember to ask it later.

9. If your narrator does stray into subjects that are not pertinent (the most common problems are to follow some family member's children or to get into a series of family medical problems), try to pull her back as quickly as possible. "Before we move on, I'd like to find out how the closing of the mine in 1935 affected your family's finances. Do you remember that?"

10. It is often hard for a narrator to describe people. An easy way to begin is to ask her to describe the person's appearance. From there, the narrator is more likely to move into character description.

11. Interviewing is one time when a negative approach is more effective than a positive one. Ask about the negative aspects of a situation. For example, in asking about a person, do not begin with a

glowing description. "I know the mayor was a very generous and wise person. Did you find him so?" Few narrators will quarrel with a statement like that even though they may have found the mayor a disagreeable person. You will get a more lively answer if you start out in the negative. "Despite the mayor's reputation for good works, I hear he was a very difficult man for his immediate employees to get along with." If your narrator admired the mayor greatly, she will spring to his defense with an apt illustration of why your statement is wrong. If she did find him hard to get along with, your remark has given her a chance to illustrate some of the mayor's more unpleasant characteristics.

12. Try to establish at every important point in the story where the narrator was or what her role was in this event, in order to indicate how much is eye-witness information and how much based on reports of others. "Where were you at the time of the mine disaster?" "Did you talk to any of the survivors later?" Work around these questions carefully, so that you will not appear to be doubting the accuracy of the narrator's account.

13. Do not challenge accounts you think may be inaccurate. Instead, try to develop as much information as possible that can be used by later researchers in establishing what probably happened. Your narrator may be telling you quite accurately what she saw. As Walter Lord explained when describing his interviews with survivors of the *Titanic*, "Every lady I interviewed had left the sinking ship in the last lifeboat. As I later found out from studying the placement of the lifeboats, no group of lifeboats was in view of another and each lady probably *was* in the last lifeboat she could see leaving the ship."

14. Tactfully point out to your narrator that there is a different account of what she is describing, if there is. Start out by saying, "I have heard . . ." or "I have read . . ." This is not a challenge to her account, but rather an opportunity for her to bring up further evidence to refute the opposing view, or to explain how that view got established, or to temper what she has already said. If done skillfully, some of your best information can come from this juxtaposition of differing accounts.

15. Try to avoid "off the record" information—the times when your narrator asks you to turn off the recorder while she tells you a good story. Ask her to let you record the whole thing and promise that you will erase that portion if she asks you to after further consideration. You may have to erase it later, or she may not tell you the story

at all, but once you allow "off the record" stories, she may continue with more and more, and you will end up with almost no recorded interview at all. "Off the record" information is only useful if you yourself are researching a subject and this is the only way you can get the information. It has no value if your purpose is to collect information for later use by other researchers.

16. Don't switch the recorder off and on. It is much better to waste a little tape on irrelevant material than to call attention to the tape recorder by a constant on-off operation. For this reason, I do not recommend the stop-start switches available on some mikes. If your mike has such a switch, tape it to the "on" position to avoid an inadvertent missing of material—then forget it. Of course you can turn off the recorder if the telephone rings or someone interrupts your session.

17. Interviews usually work out better if there is no one present except the narrator and the interviewer. Sometimes two or more narrators can be successfully recorded, but usually each one of them would have been better alone.

18. End the interview at a reasonable time. An hour and a half is

probably the maximum. First, you must protect your narrator against over-fatigue; second, you will be tired even if she isn't. Some narrators tell you very frankly if they are tired, or their spouses will. Otherwise, *you* must plead fatigue, another appointment, or no more tape.

19. Don't use the interview to show off your own knowledge, vocabulary, charm, or other abilities. Good interviewers do not shine; only their interviews do.

Indexing

Tapes

It is most efficient to index the tape shortly after you return from the interview. Tapes can be indexed by time segments, such as five-minute intervals. While most tape recorders have an index counter, often called a digital counter, our experience is that these are not standard and that tape indexes prepared according to the count on one machine are not accurate on another machine, nor even on the same machine a year later. I therefore recommend a time-segment index. This can be prepared by listening through the tape, watching a clock, and writing down the major topic of discussion during each five- to ten-minute segment. For example:

Minutes

00	Born 1910. Brothers and sisters.
07	Kringle family background, from Ohio.
09	Father's trip West in 1900.
12	Farming in Central County, wheat, pests, depression of 1920s.
20	College days at U.C. Berkeley, class of 1931.
	Professors, students, social life.
28	Return to Central City, job in uncle's bank, Depression.
	Second side of tape
00	Banking regulations of 1930s, farm foreclosures.
10	World War II, North Africa and Italy.
20	Baby boom, 1946.

Include with the index, and file with the tape, a list of names (correctly spelled), dates, hard-to-hear phrases or old-fashioned phrases, and other information that will assist the researcher at a future time. A sample sheet for a tape index used for the Bancroft Library's Donated Oral Histories Collection follows.

Donated Oral Histories Collection
Regional Oral History Office

The Bancroft Library
University of California
Berkeley, California 94720

General Topic of Interview ⎯⎯⎯⎯⎯⎯⎯⎯⎯⎯⎯⎯⎯⎯⎯⎯⎯⎯

Date ⎯⎯⎯⎯⎯⎯⎯⎯⎯⎯⎯⎯⎯⎯⎯⎯⎯⎯⎯⎯⎯⎯⎯⎯⎯⎯⎯⎯⎯⎯⎯

Place ⎯⎯⎯⎯⎯⎯⎯⎯⎯⎯⎯⎯⎯⎯⎯⎯⎯⎯⎯⎯⎯⎯⎯⎯⎯⎯⎯⎯⎯⎯⎯

Length ⎯⎯⎯⎯⎯⎯⎯⎯⎯⎯⎯⎯⎯⎯⎯⎯⎯⎯⎯⎯⎯⎯⎯⎯⎯⎯⎯⎯⎯⎯

Personal Data:

Narrator

Name ⎯⎯⎯⎯⎯⎯⎯⎯⎯⎯⎯⎯⎯⎯

Address ⎯⎯⎯⎯⎯⎯⎯⎯⎯⎯⎯⎯

⎯⎯⎯⎯⎯⎯⎯⎯⎯⎯⎯⎯⎯⎯⎯⎯⎯

Name, address of relative, friend

⎯⎯⎯⎯⎯⎯⎯⎯⎯⎯⎯⎯⎯⎯⎯⎯⎯

Birthplace ⎯⎯⎯⎯⎯⎯⎯⎯⎯⎯⎯

Birthdate ⎯⎯⎯⎯⎯⎯⎯⎯⎯⎯

Occupation(s) ⎯⎯⎯⎯⎯⎯⎯

⎯⎯⎯⎯⎯⎯⎯⎯⎯⎯⎯⎯⎯⎯⎯⎯⎯⎯

⎯⎯⎯⎯⎯⎯⎯⎯⎯⎯⎯⎯⎯⎯⎯⎯⎯⎯

Interviewer

Name ⎯⎯⎯⎯⎯⎯⎯⎯⎯⎯⎯⎯⎯⎯⎯

Address ⎯⎯⎯⎯⎯⎯⎯⎯⎯⎯⎯⎯⎯

⎯⎯⎯⎯⎯⎯⎯⎯⎯⎯⎯⎯⎯⎯⎯⎯⎯⎯

Relationship to narrator
(neighbor, co-worker, etc.) ⎯⎯⎯⎯

⎯⎯⎯⎯⎯⎯⎯⎯⎯⎯⎯⎯⎯⎯⎯⎯⎯⎯

Length of acquaintance ⎯⎯⎯⎯

⎯⎯⎯⎯⎯⎯⎯⎯⎯⎯⎯⎯⎯⎯⎯⎯⎯⎯

What was the occasion of the

interview? ⎯⎯⎯⎯⎯⎯⎯⎯⎯⎯⎯⎯

Interview Data:
Side 1
Side 2
Estimated time
on tape:

Subjects covered, in approximate order (please spell out
names of persons and places mentioned)

⎯⎯⎯⎯⎯⎯⎯   ⎯⎯⎯⎯⎯⎯⎯⎯⎯⎯⎯⎯⎯⎯⎯⎯⎯⎯⎯⎯⎯⎯⎯⎯⎯

⎯⎯⎯⎯⎯⎯⎯   ⎯⎯⎯⎯⎯⎯⎯⎯⎯⎯⎯⎯⎯⎯⎯⎯⎯⎯⎯⎯⎯⎯⎯⎯⎯

⎯⎯⎯⎯⎯⎯⎯   ⎯⎯⎯⎯⎯⎯⎯⎯⎯⎯⎯⎯⎯⎯⎯⎯⎯⎯⎯⎯⎯⎯⎯⎯⎯

⎯⎯⎯⎯⎯⎯⎯   ⎯⎯⎯⎯⎯⎯⎯⎯⎯⎯⎯⎯⎯⎯⎯⎯⎯⎯⎯⎯⎯⎯⎯⎯⎯

⎯⎯⎯⎯⎯⎯⎯   ⎯⎯⎯⎯⎯⎯⎯⎯⎯⎯⎯⎯⎯⎯⎯⎯⎯⎯⎯⎯⎯⎯⎯⎯⎯

⎯⎯⎯⎯⎯⎯⎯   ⎯⎯⎯⎯⎯⎯⎯⎯⎯⎯⎯⎯⎯⎯⎯⎯⎯⎯⎯⎯⎯⎯⎯⎯⎯

⎯⎯⎯⎯⎯⎯⎯   ⎯⎯⎯⎯⎯⎯⎯⎯⎯⎯⎯⎯⎯⎯⎯⎯⎯⎯⎯⎯⎯⎯⎯⎯⎯

Use back of sheet if necessary

Transcripts

If you transcribe, it is possible to prepare an alphabetical index of names and subjects. Index people, places, and subjects, but only if there is some real information about them in the transcript. Do not index "Herbert Hoover" if the information is "I remember as a kid I saw Herbert Hoover as he came through town on a campaign trip. It was quite a thrill to wave at the President of the United States, and I was sure he waved back." The historian looking up fresh information on Herbert Hoover will only be irritated to have spent the time to consult that tape. Good indexing requires some discrimination. A complete index may be as useless as it is impressive looking.

The Oral History Collection

Keep an index of your interviews by name of narrator, geographic area discussed, and major subjects covered in the interviews. This is the guide researchers will consult first. They may be looking up "banking" or "Central City." A quick look through the files will lead them to the Kringle interview; another look at the Kringle interview index will indicate whether it is worthwhile to listen to that tape or read that transcript. Most researchers have a limited amount of time to go through a vast amount of material; indexes of all sorts should be prepared in order to guide researchers most rapidly to whatever they are searching for.

```
Kringle, John P.          Central City banker, 1915-65

Interviewed by William Smith
Central City Historical Society, 1987

Cassette. 50 mins.  vol. K-1-69  no. 1 of 5

April 17, 1987 at Kringle home, East Hampton Street

Open.   Transcribed. 1 vol. pp. 1-46

Contents:  family background, education, early banking
practices, reaction to war-time economy, banks during Great
Depression, bank merger, move into present bank headquarters.

(See also: Banking, Central City Trust Co., Great Depression)
```

Making Information about Oral History Interviews Available to Researchers

The society's job of making oral history interviews available to researchers is not completed when the sought-for information has been captured on tape or transcript and has been indexed for easy use. The bottleneck has always been that researchers and writers have no means of knowing what rich resources on their topics might exist in the oral history collections of historical societies or libraries. One modest way to publicize the existence of oral history materials is to exchange information with other similar historical materials centers, both those in the region (for regional historians) and those that emphasize the same subject, such as agriculture, maritime history, or crafts. This can be done by sending out lists of the oral history accessions for the year with a brief listing of subjects covered in each interview, and by requesting the other institutions to send their lists in return. Such lists can be kept on file and made available to researchers who come into the society. Most major oral history offices publish catalogs of their holdings, and these should also be collected. The Oral History Association *Newsletter* is the best guide to such catalogs.

A number of states and some larger multi-state regions have prepared directories of oral history resources within their region. The directories may simply list oral history programs organized by county and city, with some reference to the subjects the program collects and the size of the collection. A few provide more details (for example, *Louisiana—Oral History Collections—A Directory, 1980*) by listing individual interviews by name of narrator. The Southwest Oral History Association (Arizona, New Mexico, Nevada, and Southern California) takes the next and most useful step for encouraging research use; the association's *Oral History Collections in the Southwest Region*, 1986, also indexes subjects covered by the oral histories and the data base is on a computer. It can be kept up-to-date, and it is accessible by computer.

Local historical societies can hook into whatever oral history directory services may exist in their region, or, if there are none, they can work with their own state library to launch such a program. Again, the Oral History Association can advise societies as to the appropriate regional oral history association for guidance.

To Transcribe or Not to Transcribe

Much can be said for transcribing and against it. Each historical society will have to weigh the pros and cons and then make its own decision on whether or not to transcribe.

For Transcribing

1. The transcribed interview, corrected by the interviewer and the narrator and indexed by names and subjects, is much easier for researchers to use than an audio tape. Researchers can skim through a transcript faster than they can listen, even selectively, to a tape. The transcript will therefore get more use.

2. A corrected transcript may be more accurate and complete because the recorded words were put down in writing while the narrator was still available to clear up obscurities. Words that are hard to hear can be checked by the actual speaker; questions that were inadequately answered can be expanded by written comment.

3. The historical society will have something visible to show for its effort. A copy for the narrator is a rich reward for her participation in the project.

Against Transcribing

1. Time and cost. Some special equipment will be needed. The historical society can expect to expend an average of six to twelve typing hours for each hour of recording. This will result in a rough transcript; in order to look nice and be most easily used, the rough transcript should be retyped after it has been corrected. It should be indexed. All these steps are as time-consuming as they are useful. Use of word-processing equipment will make the process quicker and cheaper.

2. If you transcribe you must give a copy of the interview to the narrator for her corrections. This will require further negotiations.

She may insist on rewriting the whole thing. If you do not transcribe, after you have completed the recording and your brief index of what is on the tape, the job is finished. If you transcribe, you are less than halfway through after you have done the recording.

My personal recommendation—remembering that there are those who disagree—is that the historical society should start with the intention of recording only, but that as the program becomes better established, and if there are typists on the oral history committee, a cautious beginning could be made at transcribing some of the best tapes. A well-organized program with sufficiently skilled volunteers can handle transcribing, and the results will be well worth the effort. However, at no time should the tape-recording program be allowed to bog down because of the complexities of the transcribing steps. First things first.

Transcribing Equipment

Efficient, speedy transcribing requires that the transcribing machine have a full-function foot pedal (stop/start and reverse), so that the typist can work without stopping and starting the machine by hand. There are few such machines available. (We use a Dictaphone

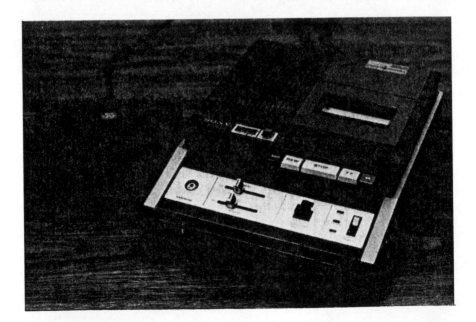

machine costing $600 and a Sanyo machine costing $300.)

Useful features to look for are automatic backup on the foot pedal (the stop/start pedal causes the tape to go backward automatically and repeat a few words of the previous section) and variable speed control (the tape can be slowed down slightly). The wear and tear of constant backward and forward action necessitates frequent repair calls. Look for a machine that comes with a maintenance agreement and quick repair service. Do not expect a machine to be able to handle 90 minute or 120 minute cassettes; they tangle and break.

Should the cost of a transcribing machine be prohibitive, it is possible, but time-consuming, to use a regular tape recorder for transcribing.

Tape recorders that come with a remote stop and start microphone can be fitted with a stop and start foot-pedal, but not with reverse. Several cassette recorders have back-space review buttons which, although operated by hand, make those machines fairly convenient for transcribing.

Transcribing Time

It takes an average of six to twelve hours to transcribe a one-hour tape. This will vary a great deal depending on the speaker and the acoustical conditions of the tape and, of course, on the skill of the transcriber. Much background noise, a person who speaks with a foreign accent, a complicated subject, a machine-gun delivery, a narrator who has suffered a stroke—any of these factors may increase the transcribing time up to fifteen hours per hour of tape.

Who Should Transcribe?

Transcribing is a challenging, interesting task that requires more than average secretarial abilities. Good typing is less essential than a sharp mind. The transcriber should have a broad general background, be able to spell, and know how to punctuate so as to catch the meaning of the spoken word. Improper punctuation can completely change the meaning of a series of words. The transcriber must have the discrimination to determine from the context which word to type when several words sound similar, when to leave in an incomplete sentence because it is important and when to leave it out because the narrator just made a false start, when to include editorial remarks such as "(sarcastic laughter)." A keen ear for electronic sound is essential; some people just can't hear sound very well from a tape recorder.

Method of Transcribing

Transcribe almost verbatim, but listen ahead sufficiently to leave out false starts, fumbling for the correct word, coffee-time conversation (unless it is pertinent), or too many "you know's" or "rights?" Retain the speech characteristics of the narrator, but do not try to spell out phonetically unusual pronunciations such as "yup" for "yes." Do not improve grammar or syntax.

In the interest of an uninterrupted narrative, some transcribers try to eliminate the interviewer's questions. This gives a false picture of why the narrator said what she said. Retain the questions.

Leave a blank for unintelligible portions, noting down in pencil the approximate point on the tape where this occurred. The interviewer will probably be able to listen through and catch it. Try to approximate the spelling of spoken names; again, the interviewer may be able to correct them. Ideally, the interviewer will have taken notes of all names mentioned during the interview and will have asked the narrator to check them for correct spelling.

Prepare two copies of the transcript, one to keep verbatim and one to use for editing and correcting by the interviewer. After editing and before sending the edited copy to the interviewee for her review and approval, make a clear photocopy of the edited transcript to hold as your insurance copy. Interviewees have been known to lose the transcript.

Submitting the Transcript to the Narrator for Review

Do not return portions of the transcript to the narrator until the entire interview has been tape-recorded. If you return the transcript to her week by week, you will find much time is spent in revising or re-recording rather than in getting on with the story. After all of the recording is completed, the transcript can be submitted chapter by chapter (if the series was long, asking someone to correct several hundred pages would be too overwhelming) or in its entirety (if the manuscript is of manageable size for the narrator).

Ask the narrator to read the transcript carefully and to correct errors of fact or spelling, but *urge her not* to try to formalize the conversational style. Reiterate again and again, in person and by letter, that you want this to read as a conversation, that you want to retain the spontaneity of the spoken word. You may have to speak to family members as well, and you may be well advised to stop by her house to see what she is doing with the transcript if she keeps it too long. Many narrators, especially of the older generation, find it almost impossible to resist revising their transcripts into what they think would have been an acceptable essay for their high-school English teachers.

Agreements on Use

A Pre-recording Understanding

It is wise to have written evidence of the narrator's understanding of the purpose and procedures of the program and of her agreement to permit the use of her interviews for historical research. First, although you probably will have talked to her in person and will have explained the whole program, write her a letter explaining again why you are doing the recording, what the procedure will be, and make it clear that these tapes will be available for historical research. At the Bancroft Library, we send the narrator two copies of this letter and ask her to sign one and return it to us if the plan as outlined meets her approval. You may not want to be that formal, but at least have on file a carbon of the letter you sent her.

The Agreement on Use

As soon as you have completed all of the recording, have the narrator sign an agreement on use. The simpler the agreement, the better. Many narrators are frightened by complex and legalistic releases.

Have the rights to use turned over to an organization that can be expected to exist for a long time—most likely the historical society. If this is a temporary oral history program, the city or county library may be the most appropriate depository and owner.

The transfer of rights should include also the transfer of any rights the interviewer may have in the oral history.

The wording of a simple agreement for the Central City History Society is included here as a sample.

Ask Permission to Use a Substantial Portion of the Interview

If it is planned to use any substantial portion of an interview in a public way, say, in a newspaper or a historical monument pamphlet, it is common courtesy to ask the narrator for permission before using it. She will probably be pleased. But if she doesn't want it used, no

Central City Historical Society
85 Main Street
Central City, Missouri

We, _____(narrator)_____ and _____(interviewer)_____ , do hereby give to the Central City Historical Society for such scholarly and educational uses as the Director of the Central City Historical Society shall determine the following tape-recorded interview(s) recorded on _____(dates)_____ as an unrestricted gift and transfer to the Central City Historical Society legal title and all literary property rights including copyright. This gift does not preclude any use which we may want to make of the information in the recordings ourselves.

This agreement may be revised or amended by mutual consent of the parties undersigned.

_____
Signature of Narrator

_____

_____
Name & Address of Narrator

_____
Dated

Accepted for the Central City
Historical Society by

_____
Signature of Interviewer

_____
Chairman, Oral History Committee

_____

_____
Dated

_____
Name & Address of Interviewer

_____
Dated

_____

Subject of Interview(s)

matter how generous she has been in signing over all rights to the society, *do not use it*. Nothing will damage an oral history program as much as a disgruntled narrator who feels her material has been used improperly.

Restricting Material

Very occasionally a narrator will divulge some information that she wishes "put under seal" (that is, closed to all use) for a certain number of years or which the interviewer feels should be under seal. This can be handled in the signed agreement by a sentence added to the usual statement. This is the sentence used by the Bancroft Library:

Limitation on publication. The parties hereto agree that pages 14-16 of the manuscript and the portions of the tape from which these pages were transcribed shall not be published or otherwise made available to anyone other than the parties hereto until January 1, 1999.

Work out with the narrator a reasonable time limitation based upon why she wishes it placed under seal. It may be "during the lifetime of the narrator" or a date when all the persons involved can be presumed to have died.

Alternatives other than "open" or "sealed" are "closed during the narrator's lifetime except with the narrator's permission" or "open only with the permission of the president of the society."

Our one experience with "closed during the narrator's lifetime except with her permission" was unfortunate. The narrator's purpose in placing the limitation had been that she personally wanted to meet the scholars who were working on her topic, just for fun and because she felt she would surely be able to answer some of their questions specifically and in greater detail than she had in her interview. Alas, the narrator lived on for many years in a condition of poor health which made it impossible for her to grant permission; the interview was therefore closed until her death. Several Ph.D. theses were written during this time on subjects she had discussed, but none could incorporate her comments.

By all means avoid any transferring of discretion over use of the interview to heirs. Let the narrators make up their own minds on when to open the material.

Closed Is Closed

Whatever the agreement, it must be adhered to rigidly.

If the interview is to be put under seal, pack into a box the tape, the notes about the interview, and the tape index, tie it securely, seal it with wax, mark on the outside the date when it can be opened, and put it away in a safe place. A card indicating generally what the tape is about, but not specifically what the closed material is, can be kept in the society's oral history files. It should be marked "closed until 1999" or "closed until five years after Mrs. A. B. Doe's death" or whatever the restriction is.

The interviewer, and the transcriber if the interview was transcribed, must also adhere to the agreement by not talking about the closed information. "I am sorry but Mrs. Doe has closed her interview until 1999" should be the end of any conversation about it.

Discourage Restricted Material

In most instances the focus of the oral history program is such that there is no reason to collect material that must be closed. Except in the few cases where sensitive material is really pertinent, the closing of material should be discouraged. If interviews are not transcribed, a few closed sentences mean the whole tape becomes inaccessible for a period of time. If the material is transcribed, only the sensitive pages and the tape need to be sealed; the rest of the transcript can be open. However, this still necessitates a foolproof on-going system of keeping the material closed and then of opening it on the appointed date. The operation of an active oral history program will involve enough details without adding one more of such long duration.

Ethics of Oral History

The value and continuation of oral history interviewing depend upon the voluntary ethical conduct of oral history practitioners, and upon the ability of oral history projects to abide by their agreements over whatever period of time is stipulated.

Responsibility to the Narrator

It is the responsibility of the oral history practitioner to deal fairly in every respect. The value of the interviews that will be conducted with the narrator depends upon the confidence she has in the interviewer, in the reputation of the historical society, and in the reputation of the entire field of oral history. The members of an oral history project have the following responsibilities to the narrator:

1. To make clear to the narrator what the process will be at each step, how the material will be handled, and what restrictions she can place upon it.

2. To get down what happened as accurately as possible, and to this end to work together with the narrator to record the information. This will include developing delicate or controversial material (where relevant) in such a way as to give the narrator the fullest opportunity to record her point of view.

3. To advise her, with her interests in mind, as to what the best agreement on use would be. If, in your opinion, something she said could be used in a way damaging to her, advise her to put it under seal. It will be of no benefit to the oral history program to have a narrator's reputation damaged through something she said in an oral history interview.

4. To adhere to any agreement made.

Responsibility to the Historical Profession

Every effort should be made to maintain the good reputation of oral history as a field by keeping faith with the narrators. In addition, the oral history materials produced should be made as useful to researchers as possible. This includes:

49

1. Produce the best interviews you can.
2. Make a typescript, if at all possible.
3. Index the tapes or transcripts.
4. Make the existence of your oral history materials known.
5. Make it possible for researchers to use the materials (unless they are under seal).

Oral History Association Goals and Guidelines

The Oral History Association by unanimous approval adopted the following statement on November 25, 1968, with minor revisions since then.

Goals and Guidelines
of the Oral History Association

The Oral History Association recognizes oral history as a method of gathering and preserving historical information in spoken form and encourages those who produce and use oral history to recognize certain principles, rights, and obligations for the creation of source material that is authentic, useful, and reliable.

Guidelines for the Interviewee

The interviewee should be informed of the purposes and procedures of oral history in general and of the particular project to which contribution is being made.

In recognition of the importance of oral history to an understanding of the past and in recognition of the costs and effort involved, the interviewee should strive to impart candid information of lasting value.

The interviewee should be aware of the mutual rights involved in oral history, such as editing and seal privileges, literary rights, prior use, fiduciary relationships, royalties, and determination of the disposition of all forms of the record and extent of dissemination and use.

Preferences of the person interviewed and any prior agreements should govern the conduct of the oral history process, and these preferences and agreements should be carefully documented for the record.

Guidelines for the Interviewer

Interviewers should guard against possible social injury to or exploitation of interviewees and should conduct interviews with respect for human dignity.

Each interviewee should be selected on the basis of demonstrable potential for imparting information of lasting value.

The interviewer should strive to prompt informative dialogue through challenging and perceptive inquiry, should be grounded in the background and experiences of the person being interviewed, and, if possible, should review the sources relating to the interviewee before conducting the interview.

Interviewers should extend the inquiry beyond their immediate needs to make each interview as complete as possible for the benefit of others, and should, wherever possible, place the material in a depository where it will be available for general research.

The interviewer should inform the interviewee of the planned conduct of the oral history process and develop mutual expectations of rights connected thereto, including editing, mutual seal privileges, literary rights, prior use, fiduciary relationships, royalties, rights to determine disposition of all forms of the record, and the extent of dissemination and use.

Interviews should be conducted in a spirit of objectivity, candor and integrity, and in keeping with common understandings, purposes and stipulations mutually arrived at by all parties.

The interviewer shall not violate and will protect the seal on any information considered confidential by the interviewee, whether imparted on or off the record.

Guidelines for Sponsoring Institutions

Subject to conditions prescribed by interviewees, it is an obligation of sponsoring institutions (or individual collectors) to prepare and preserve easily usable records; to keep careful records of the creation and processing of each interview; to identify, index, and catalog interviews; and, when open to research, to make their existence known.

Interviewers should be selected on the basis of professional competence and interviewing skill; interviewers should be carefully matched to interviewees.

Institutions should keep both interviewees and interviewers aware of the importance of the above guidelines for the successful production and use of oral history sources.

Legal Restrictions

There are few legal restrictions that limit the collection and publication of historical materials. Slander or libel are the ones most likely to be of concern to oral historians. Slander is the oral or written defamation of a person by means of a false report, maliciously uttered, which injures the reputation of the person. Libel is defamation by the publication of this kind of false utterance, without just cause, and which tends to expose the other to public hatred, contempt, or ridicule.

Various court cases have progressively reduced the possibility of a court finding any historical effort either slanderous or libelous. First, the dead cannot be libeled. Second, libelous defamation of prominent living persons must include actual malice plus irresponsible disregard for the truth.

The interviewer may need to be a little more concerned if his questioning leads him into the purely private lives of people, although he still has a good defense if he can indicate this is truth published for good motives. Of course, there always exists the possibility of harassment in the lower courts through filing of suits for defamation. Such suits stand almost no possibility of ending in a court award for damages, but they could cost time and expense to the interviewer or the project in defending themselves. But to all intents and purposes, slander or libel is a nonexistent danger to an oral history project.

The question of literary property rights is a little more complicated, and court cases have not been numerous enough nor consistent enough to serve as guides to oral historians. Therefore, the best advice is to get a proper, signed release for use of all interviews, and then to go to the added courtesy of getting specific permission for publication of any substantial portions. It is better to err on the side of asking for too many permissions than to damage good public relations of the society.

Depositing and Preserving Tapes

Because the basic purpose of oral history is to capture accounts of the past in a permanent form and to make that information available to present and future users, it should go without saying that the oral histories must go into a library. In reality, too many oral history efforts, either by individual researchers or by ad hoc groups, never get to that last step of the tapes and transcripts being deposited in a library. Instead, the oral histories are filed away in a desk drawer, perhaps awaiting the writing of the book the individual or group expected to publish, then forgotten, and eventually lost. Depositing the oral histories is an essential step in the process.

Where to Deposit Tapes

Two considerations should govern where you deposit the tapes:
1. Long-term safety and preservation
2. Accessibility for research
If the historical society has a relatively fireproof building or perma-

nent location, if its library or museum is open on a regular basis for a reasonable number of hours weekly, and if the society seems to be a permanent organization able to meet long-term commitments, then by all means keep the tapes and other related manuscripts right there. If, however, the society's office is in the living room of the current president, or, while it has a permanent building, it is open only two afternoons a week, then consider the local library as a more accessible place in which to deposit the tapes and manuscripts for use by the public. In a smaller community, it would be logical for the historical society and the library to share the responsibility of working on local history—the society collecting papers, producing oral history interviews, and managing the museum or historic sites; the library preserving and servicing the manuscript and oral history materials.

Sometimes it is suggested that, in order to facilitate research, the oral history interviews should be deposited in a central depository such as the state historical society or a university or state library. Assuming that the interview material is primarily local in nature, it would seem more important for the researcher to work right in the community in order to use other papers there and to get the feel of the area. The prime users will probably be community residents, who would find travel to an out-to-town depository an inconvenience.

Storage and Handling of Tapes

Cassettes, convenient as they are for recording and playback, are not good for permanent storage of tapes. If at all possible, plan to re-record your prize tapes onto 7-inch reels, 1-1/2 mil mylar tape, to hold as your archival tape. This means the archive must have a 7-inch reel playback machine, too. The original cassette or copies can be used for patron listening. If reel-to-reel equipment is not available, hold the original cassette as the archival copy, and make a copy for patron use. The following rules are applicable to reels or cassettes.

1. Store tapes under "people conditions." Ideal "people conditions" are ideal tape use and storage conditions. In broad terms this means a fairly constant temperature in the 70s, and a relative humidity of about 50 percent. If the tapes are subjected to extreme cold or heat, do not listen to them until they have had at least twenty-four hours to stablize at good "people conditions." Do not use artificial means to hasten this stabilization period.

2. Handle in a "clean room" environment. Dust and lint can damage tapes when they are used, so strive for a "clean-room" environment in the listening area. Do not eat, drink, or smoke when tapes are handled. Smoke will not damage the tapes but fine ashes will. Avoid getting fingerprints on the tapes, and do not use grease or wax pencil to mark them; these will only attract and hold dust particles.

3. Store in the original box. Tapes should be stored in the cardboard or plastic containers they came in, standing on edge on a shelf. The containers can be placed in a plastic bag for additional protection against dust and moisture.

4. Wind the tape evenly. Before storing the tape, run it though the recorder at "play" speed, not "fast forward" or "rewind". Rewind it occasionally at "play" to relieve strains and adhesions before they seriously affect the tape.

5. Avoid stray magnetic fields. Avoid accidental exposure to magnetic fields from electric generators or motors, as such exposure can lead to print-through or complete erasure. Do not store tapes near a steady field of DC current, a permanent magnet, or a concentrated field of AC current. And avoid magnetic catches on the cupboards in the tape storage room.

6. Clean the tape recorder periodically.

Allowing People to Use the Tapes

Do not permit tapes to be taken out of the depository for listening or other uses unless you retain the original and have a copy that can be lent out. You should have a tape recorder and earphones available in the depository for people to use for listening. The recorder should be kept clean so the tapes will not be damaged.

Of course it is possible to erase a tape by pushing the "record" button. As a precaution, the tabs in the back of the cassettes should be pushed out so that the tapes cannot be erased by error. If the cassette recorder in the depository is to be used only for listening, it is cheaper and safer to get a play-back-only machine. Reel recorders can have a lock put on the record button so it cannot be activated.

Encouraging the Use
of Oral History Materials

Stimulate Use

So far we have been discussing the first and major role of the oral history committee, that of getting information onto tape and then of indexing it and making it available for use. A second responsibility is to try to get the tapes or transcripts into use now. It is only through feed-back from users that the committee has any way to measure the value of the interviews. Having the material used will please the narrators (if it doesn't, don't use it yet), publicize the program, and raise the morale of the oral history committee. So do put some effort into finding ways to use the material soon. Some possible immediate uses follow.

Historical Research

The primary use, of course, is for historical research, and most of this will be in the future. It will be many years before you know how well your efforts have worked out. Of one thing you may be certain: no user will be satisfied with your interviews; each will wish you had spent more time on the subject of his or her special concern and had not wasted your time on subjects he or she is not interested in. In trying to out-guess the future, aim at a well-rounded interview with emphasis on what the narrator can tell best.

Many interviews will fit in with the current research interests of members of the historical society. By all means encourage local researchers to participate in the interviewing, have them submit questions to be asked that will provide information for their research, and publicize what interviews you have so that researchers will come and use them.

Newspaper Columns on Local History

Several local historical societies report that the newspaper runs excerpts from their oral history interviews, often on some timely theme. (The opening of a new school, for example, may be the occasion for several columns on the early schools of the vicinity.) Local societies report that a local history column is especially popular with newcomers to the area. Oral history has much to offer to the many wandering Americans who attempt to sink roots into a new community.

Narrative for Slide Lectures

Well-edited excerpts from a number of interviews can provide a taped narrative for a series of slides, making a lively lecture on local history for schools or organizations.

Taped Descriptions for Museum Exhibits

Very brief excerpts, less than one minute, can be prepared as push-button descriptions of exhibits. How much more interesting to hear

an actual user of an antiquated implement explaining how it was used than to read the description on the wall.

Classroom Use

Various illustrated lectures with taped excerpts can be prepared to interest different age levels. However, a more effective use of oral history is to locate especially cooperative and stimulating narrators, then have the children prepare questions and go out and record them themselves. The preparation of the questions, the recording session, and then the presentation of the results to the class can be an invaluable experience.

Radio and Theater

Increasingly, oral history tapes are being used for radio documentaries. This requires that they will have been recorded with broadcast-quality sound. In other cases, the dialogue can be used as the basis for theater scripts. This works out especially well with community projects for which a goal is to return to the community a public presentation of their history.

Developing Expertise

Successful oral history program planning and interviewing is a skill that comes only from experience plus careful evaluation of the work that has been completed. You learn by doing, so the first step is to start doing.

Interviews—Analyze Your Own Tapes

Your first listen-through of a completed tape will be to prepare the tape index and notes and to jot down questions for the next interviewing session. Later, listen through again, this time for the sole purpose of listing questions, comments, or procedures that went well, and those that went badly. For example, "How did you feel about that?" may have gotten a good response, while "You don't say!" may have shut her up completely. Switching off the machine while you asked the narrator to pass the sugar and cream for your coffee and then switching it on again may have formalized an easy-rolling story. Assume that you are to use this tape to instruct some novices in what to do and what not to do. Here, as in asking questions about people, the negative approach is often more fruitful than the positive. While it is very hard to illustrate what to do, it is easy to see what not to do.

Committee Workshops

When several people have completed tapes, plan a workshop for just the oral history committee, or maybe for only three or four interviewers on the committee. Have each participant bring in one or two examples of errors. They may also be asked to bring in an example of a successful way out of a problem, but those are harder to illustrate (and less fun for the committee).

I recall a period in my high school years when we vied with each other in reporting our "boners." These were gross ineptitudes in handling social problems—the wrong thing said at a given moment, the stumble as one tried to make a graceful exit—and as poiseless adolescents we had plenty to report each day. It was a bit cheering as one found oneself in a mortifying situation to think about what a funny story it would make at the next "boner" session.

Regional or State Workshops

Many questions of mutual interest, which will arise among historical societies conducting oral history programs, can be very usefully discussed at meetings attended by representatives of a number of societies. The workshop could be on oral history in general, or it could be focused on any one of the considerations mentioned in this booklet. Individuals charged with various responsibilites in the oral history program could participate in the section on their specialties.

The Oral History Association

In 1967 a national association was formed of individuals interested or engaged in oral history. The Oral History Association holds an

annual colloquium in various areas of the United States. These are intensive three-day workshops of panels, lectures, discussion groups, and demonstrations on the many phases of oral history.

In addition, the Oral History Association serves as clearinghouse for information on regional oral history associations. The OHA publishes quarterly the *OHA Newsletter*, which reports on oral history developments; twice a year it publishes the *Oral History Review* with longer articles on the uses and methods of oral history, and it puts out occasional pamphlets.

Members receive current publications and can order back publications at a reduced price. Membership in OHA is a best buy for any group practicing oral history. For details, write the Oral History Association, P.O. Box 926, University Station, Lexington, Kentucky 40506-0025.

Bibliography

This is a selected bibliography of books that have the most bearing on oral history for the volunteer historical society. Addresses and prices have been listed for less accessible materials.

Oral History Manuals

Baum, Willa K. *Transcribing and Editing Oral History.* 1977, 127 pp. Nashville: American Association for State and Local History (172 Second Avenue North, Suite 102, Nashville, Tenn. 37201). $9. Comprehensive advice and examples on each step from the tape to the written record.

Charlton, Thomas L. *Oral History for Texans.* 1981, 85 pp. Austin: Texas Historical Commission (P.O. Box 12276, Austin, Texas 78711). $5.75. An excellent example of a manual slanted to the history and concerns of a state. Good advice and bibliography for oral history anywhere.

Cutting-Baker, Holly, et al. *Family Folklore Interviewing Guide and Questionnaire.* 1978, 7 pp. Washington, D.C. U.S. Government Printing Office. $1. Good ideas for questions.

Davis, Cullom, Kathryn Buck, Kay MacLean. *Oral History: From Tape to Type.* 1977, 141 pp. Chicago: American Library Association (50 East Huron St., Chicago, Ill. 60611). $9. A basic guide with style guide and library cataloging information. Presently out-of-print, but worth watching for a new edition.

Deering, Mary Jo. *Transcribing Without Tears: A Guide to Transcribing and Editing Oral History Interviews.* 1976, 38 pp. Washington, D.C.: George Washington University Library. (Oral History Program, George Washington University Library, Washington, D.C.). $2.75. An easy-to-follow guide with clear examples.

Epstein, Ellen Robinson and Rona Mendelsohn. *Record And Remember: Tracing Your Roots Through Oral History.* 1978, 119 pp. Washington, D.C. Center for Oral History, Chevy Chase, Md. (7507 Wyndale Road, Chevy Chase, Md. 20815). $4.25. Aimed at family history, especially immigrant families. Good theme questions.

Frontiers: A Journal of Women Studies, Vol. VII, No. 1, 1983, 121 pp. Special Issue: Women's Oral History Two, (*Frontiers*, Women Studies Program, University of Colorado, Boulder, Colo. 80309). $8. Eighteen articles on uses of women's oral history projects, examples of projects, listing of women's oral history projects in the U.S., sampling techniques, bibliography.

Handfield, F. Gerald, Jr. *History on Tape: A Guide for Oral History In Indiana*. 1981, 23pp. Indianapolis: Indiana State Library. (Oral History Project, 140 N. Senate Ave., Indianapolis, Ind. 46204). $.50. Brief and clear. Includes a history time line for Indiana, and a listing of oral history projects in Indiana.

Ives, Edward D. *The Tape-Recorded Interview: A Manual for Field Workers in Folklore and Oral History*. 1980, 130 pp. Knoxville: The University of Tennessee Press (Knoxville, Tenn. 37996). $7. A full and readable manual by a leading folklorist, especially strong on recording techniques. Includes samples of form letters, agreements, accession forms.

Key, Betty McKeever. *Maryland Manual of Oral History*. 1979, 47 pp. Baltimore: Maryland Historical Society (201 West Monument St., Baltimore, Md. 21201). $4. Especially good on how to organize a whole program, keep track of what you get, and apply for funding.

Kornbluh, Joyce and M. Brady Mikusko, ed. *Working Womenroots: An Oral History Primer*. 1979, 74 pp. Ann Arbor, Michigan: Institute of Labor and Industrial Relations (Ann Arbor, Mich. 48109). $3.50. A brief guide for women in labor unions. Questions are especially good for any women's history.

Lance, David. *An Archives Approach to Oral History*. 1978, 64 pp. London: Imperial War Museum (Lambeth Road, London SE1 6HZ, England). 3 pounds [$4.50]. Practical details on how to select interviewees, keep records as the project progresses. Especially good on how to encourage the use of tapes rather than transcripts.

Oblinger, Carl. *Interviewing the People of Pennsylvania*. 1978, 84 pp. Harrisburg: Pennsylvania Historical and Museum Commission (Box 1026, Harrisburg, Penn. 17120). $5.50. A thoughtful book that combines theory and method with many clear examples.

O'Hanlan, Elizabeth, O.P. *Oral History for the Religious Archives: The Sinsinawa Collection*. 1978, 63 pp. Sinsinawa Dominican Archives (Sinsinawa, Wisc. 53824). $5. Basic advice for any institution. Good examples of a tape index and a program master index.

Reimer, Derek, David Mattison and Allen W. Specht. *Voices, A Guide to Oral History*. 1984, 74 pp. Victoria: Provincial Archives, British Columbia (Sound and Moving Image Division, Provincial Archives, Victoria, British Columbia, Canada V8V 2R5). $5. An excellent manual aimed at radio broadcast quality interviews. Detailed information on equipment and recording methods. Good examples of cataloging. A best buy.

Shumway, Gary L. and William G. Hartley. *An Oral History Primer.* 1973, 28 pp. Salt Lake City: Primer Publications (P.O. Box 11894, Salt Lake City, Utah 84147). $2.50. A simple guide on how to get going, especially aimed at doing one's own family history.

Sitton, Thad, George L. Mehaffy, and O.L. Davis, Jr. *Oral History: A Guide for Teachers (and Others).* 1983, 167 pp. Austin, Texas: University of Texas Press (P.O. Box 7819, Austin, Texas 78712). $8.98. A complete guide to using oral history in the classroom as a teaching method. Many ideas are useful to the historical society as well.

Whistler, Nancy. *Oral History Workshop Guide.* 1979, 55 pp. Denver: Colorado Center for Oral History, Denver Public Library (Western History Department, Denver Public Library, 1357 Broadway, Denver, Colo. 80203). $3.50. A well-organized manual for teaching oral history by a statewide program of workshops.

Oral History in General

Allen, Barbara and Lynwood Montell. *From Memory to History: Using Oral Sources in Local Historical Research.* 1981, 176 pp. Nashville: American Association for State and Local History. $5.95. How to evaluate and use oral history to write history.

Brady, John. *The Craft of Interviewing.* 1976, 244 pp. Cincinnati, Ohio: Writers Digest Books (9933 Alliance Road, Cincinnati, Ohio 45242). $9.95. A breezy book on all kinds of interviewing techniques, many not suitable for oral history, but full of ideas both good and bad on how to get the information.

Dunaway, David K. and Willa K. Baum. *Oral History: An Interdisciplinary Anthology.* 1984, 439 pp. Nashville: American Association for State and Local History. $17.95. A collection of the best scholarly writing on oral history, its uses, promise, and problems. Not a manual, but full bibliographies following each chapter are a key to all the writings on oral history up to 1983.

Havlice, Patricia Pate. *Oral History: A Reference Guide and Annotated Bibliography.* 1985, 140 pp. Jefferson: N.C. McFarland and Co., Inc. (Box 611, Jefferson, N.C. 28640). $29.95. This 1985 bibliography gives anno-

tated entries on manuals, articles about oral history, guides to collections, and books based on oral history. A well-done subject index
enables users to find publications on their topics. Very useful, but
expensive. Look for it in the library.

Moss, William W. *Oral History Program Manual*.1974, 109 pp. New York:
Praeger Publishers. $13.50. A thoughtful consideration of how to set
up a large-scale project, based on the experiences of the John F.
Kennedy Oral History Program. Presently out-of-print. This book
is essential reading for the serious, scholarly oral historian. Look for
it in the library.

Neuenschwander, John A. *Oral History and the Law.* 1985, 24 pp. Lexington, Kentucky: Oral History Association. (P.O. Box 926, University
Station, Lexington, Kentucky 40506-0025.) $4. The latest and clearest
statement of legal considerations for oral history, written by a past-
president of the Oral History Association who is also a professor of
history and a copyright lawyer. The first of the Oral History Association's useful pamphlet series.

Oral History Association. *Evaluation Guidelines.* 1980. 14 pp. Lexington, Kentucky: Oral History Association (P.O. Box 926, University Station, Lexington, Kentucky 40506-0025). $2. Free to members. A brief booklet
encapsulating the ethics and standards of the oral history community. This is just one of the publications sent free or at reduced cost
to members of the Oral History Association. Members ($20 a year)
also receive the bi-annual *Oral History Review* and the quarterly *Oral
History Association Newsletter,* and referral to regional and state oral
history organizations.

Richardson, Stephen A., Barbara Snell Dohrenwend, and David Klein.
Interviewing: Its Forms and Functions. 1965. New York: Basic Books.
An academic text on all kinds of interviewing, including oral his-
tory. For the serious interviewer.

Seldon, Anthony and Joanna Pappworth. *By Word of Mouth.* 1983, 258 pp.
London and New York: Methuen and Co., (29 West Thirty-fifth
Street, New York, N.Y. 10001). $13. Aimed at academic research proj-
ects, this excellent and thoughtful book from England offers theory
and practical information. Required reading for the serious oral
historian.

Thompson, Paul. *The Voice of the Past: Oral History.* 1978, 257 pp. New York:
Oxford University Press. (16-00 Pullitt Drive, Fair Lawn, New Jersey
07410). $8.95. A theoretical and practical guide to oral history by
England's leading oral historian. This is the best book so far on oral
historiography.

Examples of the Use of Oral History

There are many examples of books based on oral histories; only a few are listed here. The most relevant examples are often locally printed paperbacks focusing on a town or region, or articles in newspapers and journals. Look for examples in your public library under the heading "oral history" and under names of towns and regions.

Arnold, Eleanor, editor. *Feeding Our Families, Memories of Hoosier Homemakers Series.* 1983, 153 pp. Indiana Extension Homemakers Association. (Order from Indiana Historical Society, 315 West Ohio Street, Indianapolis, Ind. 46202). $7. First in a series of paperbacks on homemaking, 1890-1930, thoughtfully selected from oral histories with hundreds of women of Indiana and other states. Excellent description of project, an introductory essay on the historical setting, and careful citation of each interviewer's and interviewee's contribution. Also available: *Party Lines, Pumps, and Privies,* 1984; *Buggies and Bad Tires,* 1985; *Cradles, Castor Oil and Courtship,* 1987; and a slide/tape show on *Voices of American Homemakers,* available for modest rental.

Blythe, Ronald. *Akenfield: Portrait of an English Village.* 1969, 287 pp. New York: Pantheon Books (201 East 50th Street, New York, N.Y. 10022). $5.95. One of the first and best books based on oral histories, a poetic study of the inhabitants of an English village. Beautifully edited, an inspiration on the kinds of subjects one can ask about and what can be done with collected interviews.

Cooper, Patricia and Norma Bradley Buferd. *The Quilters: Women and Domestic Art, An Oral History.* 1977, 157 pp. Garden City, New York: Anchor Press, Doubleday. $15.95. A beautiful book of photographs and oral history selections about the significance of quilts and quilting to the women of Texas and New Mexico.

Hareven, Tamara and Rudolph Langenbach. *Amoskeag: Life and Work in an American Factory-city.* 1978, 394 pp. New York: Pantheon Books (201 East 50th Street, New York, N.Y. 10022). $6.95. Oral histories from the women and men who worked in the largest textile mill in the world, Amoskeag Company of Manchester, New Hampshire, 1838-1936. Set in their historical context.

Ornstein, Barbara, editor. *Tod's Point, An Oral History.* 1981, 100 pp. Greenwich, Connecticut: Oral History Project, Friends of the Greenwich Library (Greenwich, Conn. 06830). $7.50. A history of the changing uses of a neck of land in Greenwich Cove, 1889-1980. Excerpts from

70 oral histories have been skillfully edited to create a stirring, personalized story that mirrors East Coast society from the Victorian Era through two world wars, the Great Depression, the post-war housing shortage to the 1980s when Tod's Point, now Greenwich Point, serves as a popular beach park. There are maps, photographs, a chronology, brief biographies of all the narrators, recognition of the interviewers, and a useful index. All modestly printed and paperbound. A perfect model for the local historical society.

Pennsylvania Heritage, A Magazine of Pennsylvania History and Culture. Harrisburg: Pennsylvania Historical and Museum Commission (Box 1026, Harrisburg, Pa. 17120). Year subscription, $5.50; single copy, $1.50. This historical quarterly always includes one article based on an oral history project. They are excellent examples of combining oral histories with historical context to create very readable material. Worth subscribing to even if Pennsylvania history is not your interest.

Terkel, Studs. *Hard Times: An Oral History of the Great Depression.* 1970, 462 pp. New York: Pantheon Books. $6.95. A landmark use of oral history, excerpts from interviews with the great, the notorious, and the unknown. An example of documenting a theme rather than a region.